THE DETACHMENT MANIFESTO

ALSO BY PARTH SAWHNEY

The Daily Apple

Thriving in the New Normal

The Way of the Karma Yogi

Elevation

Becoming a Karma Yogi

The Daily Learner Series

PARTH SAWHNEY

The Detachment Manifesto

Published by Parth Sawhney

THE DETACHMENT MANIFESTO

First published in 2021

Printed and bound by Draft2Digital, LLC

Contents

For my father Umesh Sawhney, who always stood by me and showered me with his love and support.

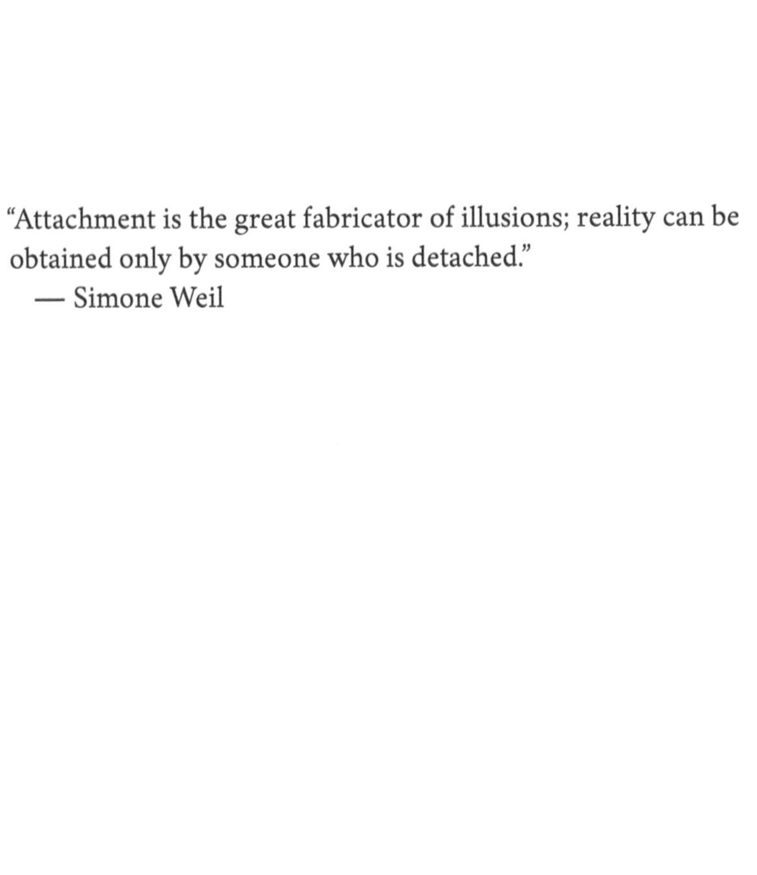

"Attachment is the great fabricator of illusions; reality can be obtained only by someone who is detached."

— Simone Weil

Introduction

Why I Wrote This Book?

Every era comes with its own difficulties. Although we are living in the best age that humanity has ever seen, the trade-off is that we have become more susceptible to falling prey to the attachments and addictions around us. Getting attached and becoming addicted is human. It happens to all of us. But the sad part is that attachments and addictions stop us from decoding our mission in our lives and unlocking our true human potential. Due to our clinging behaviors, we welcome confusion and darkness in our lives.

What I have realized in my life so far is that letting go is an important behavior that we all need to cultivate. It is not easy to change patterns overnight, but we need to take slow and steady steps to overcome them. Sometimes, in spite of our actions, we keep coming back to the same patterns and manifesting the same results. In those cases, we can bring change in ourselves in two steps:

1. Seek alignment and understand the reasons why we want to change or let go of our toxic behaviors. What are the

positive aspects of bringing this change?

2. Take action in baby steps. Massive action (or non-action) may be required in some cases, which may mean stopping the behavior cold turkey. This may not be easy, but sometimes we need to take extreme actions if all our previous attempts have failed.

As we are tempted to go back to our previous well-established behavioral patterns, the alignment that we ingrained in ourselves will help us cruise through those storms. As you can see, it is essential to seek alignment while we are struggling with our addictive behaviors because this will lay the foundation for the change in presence of aberrant patterns, strengthening our inner power.

I chose a life of minimalism, essentialism, Stoicism, Karma Yoga and detachment, and I'm glad I made this powerful change in my life. The rewards have been long-lasting and the best dividend for me has been the peace of mind that has come with it.

I am writing this book to share with you my insights and be able to guide you step-by-step in the journey that we need to take from a life of imprisonment to a life of freedom.

Detachment in the Modern World

The current world in which we are living now is a world of access. Never before in the history of humanity has it become so much easier to acquire things. Just a click of few buttons, maybe a phone call, and you can get whatever you want. Due to this ease, the most important aspect of our lives that we need to pay attention to are the kind of choices we make. It has become easy for us to become enticed and tricked. The best antidote to be able to live peacefully in this era of access is detachment. Temptations are everywhere and nowadays people in technology companies are getting paid to steal our attention. Digital dictatorships are emerging, and our limited and most precious resources — our time, presence and attention — are in jeopardy.

Getting hooked, attached and addicted has become easier than ever. The marketers know the ins and outs of the human brain, and in order to protect ourselves, our money and our invaluable resources, we need to learn how to detach from the seductive forces around us. Detachment is no longer an option for us, but it has become a necessity. Each of us is hooked and addicted to few things that we know are bad for our health and detrimental to our essential trifecta: body, mind, and spirit. The health revolution is shifting gradually from training of the body to training of the mind. A big reason for this is the information overload that we all are facing.

Detachment does not mean building walls around us and staying aloof and away from everyone. We don't need to dig ourselves into a hole, but we need to find healthier ways to experience and become whole. It means gaining wisdom to discern and decide what's best for us and focus on essentialism.

Superfluous is quickly becoming the norm, and detachment is the one and the only thing that will set us free. Building healthy boundaries and focusing on the long-term gains, instead of instant gratification, is what will take us far. It has become essential and crucial for us to cultivate a discipline of detachment so that we can maintain our well-being and embrace perennial happiness.

The Benefits of Detachment

Detachment may not be an easy road for us, but when we look at the benefits that come with it, we start realizing that embarking on this journey is worth all the ephemeral pain and discomfort that we will go through. The pains associated with detachment come in ounces, but the long-term benefits and rewards come in tons. A discussion of the benefits will help us in getting educated and enlightened so that we are able to kindle inspiration within us to choose and commit to a life of detachment. Here are some of the benefits that we can experience in this epic journey.

- Lightness: The primary benefit of letting go, whether it be in terms of physical stuff, emotional attachments or addictions is that we let go of the baggage that has been weighing us down all along. The non-essentials and junk are disposed of and we get a clear sight of our values, our passions and the direction that we need to go to. We are no longer anchored, but instead, we get grounded in positivity and authenticity. And with this groundedness, we experience freedom.
- Freedom: Freedom is the culmination of detachment. In today's age, it's easy to become a slave to other peoples' needs and wants and let society dictate our way of life. Mundane and monotony are the norm with little space left to love and live. With detachment, we gain the freedom

that seemed distant and unattainable previously. With this newly acquired freedom, we get a chance to start again with a clean slate. It becomes easier to bring big shifts and changes in our lives that we had built resistance to. With withering excuses, complaints and limiting beliefs, our freedom gives us a second chance at living a life that is happier and healthier and a lifestyle that we truly deserve.

- New experiences: With detachment, all aspects of our lives improve and the freedom allows us to soar to new heights. We start believing in a new reality for us, hence attracting new experiences in our lives. We have more time and energy in our hands that we can allot to pursuing our passions and activities that we enjoy. We choose a life of worthwhile pursuits and invest in better ways to experience life.
- Flexibility: The downside of conditioning ourselves whether on a micro or macro scale is that we make our life rigid. As our lives get filled with unnecessary obligations, attachments, unhelpful addictions, irrelevant tasks and energy vampires, we become a puppet motioned by demons that don't serve us. A great advantage of getting detached and cutting off the strings is that we become flexible. Sure, there is disruption when we switch lanes or make some changes in our lives but it is oftentimes minimal, temporary, and manageable. Flexibility is a great virtue to have when the times are trying and difficult. And that's when detachment proves to be an instrumental tool.
- A life of intention and purpose: Detachment can prove to be an essential ingredient to the recipe of living your legend and fulfilling your purpose. When we let go of the non-essentials and fluff, we are able to attain better focus

and clarity. When we align with our potential and cultivate passions that align with our inner being, we bring meaning to our work. With consistent practice of detachment, we are able to generate momentum that takes us towards doing work that we enjoy and adds value to people's lives, instead of doing the boring, tedious job just to earn money and buy shiny accoutrements to show our status and impress others.

- Happiness and inner peace: A life of harmony, peace, and happiness is something we all strive for. But in the smog of busyness, we lose our paths. Our attachments, clinginess to innocuous-seeming futile and costly wants, venomous desires and unfulfilling addictions succumb us to live a life of misery, pain, and suffering. When we become detached and focus on the most important things in our lives such as our health, relationships, passions, personal growth and transformation and contribution, we are able to better tune in with the happiness and peace that is already within us. We, humans, mistake pleasure for happiness. The spikes of dopamine have shorter shelf lives and deteriorate our holistic well-being and success, taking us into a downward spiral. The way to a good life is to detach from pleasure and choose profound joy instead.
- True connection: Detachment does not mean aloofness but it means distancing from toxic desires, people, and objects. There may be a temporary phase of emptiness that we need to plow through, but it gives us an important opportunity to start fresh and anew, and invite better things, joyous activities and like-minded people in our lives. Through detachment, we can reclaim our personal power and are able to discern what is good for us and what is

not. Detachment builds the foundation for meaningful connections. We invest our time and energy in connections that uplift our life. With detachment, we are also able to understand and connect with the Higher Power and the infinite intelligence within us. We are able to attain a life of better alignment and fulfillment.

- Health: When we experience freedom from the mental, physical and spiritual baggage that has been weighing us down, we choose a life of better health for ourselves. Through the lessons that we have learned, we are able to make better choices. With better choices, we rebuild our decimated self-esteem and self-image. We choose confidence over fears. We are able to cultivate new healthier habits that not only help us cope with our addictive tendencies but also help us build better and stronger selves. We choose emotional fitness, and with that, we bring other positive changes in our lives that impact our fitness in all aspects of our lives. Changing our psychological and physiological health becomes a priority and with this commitment, we are able to renew and redeem ourselves and gradually overcome the damages that we have done to ourselves. We become whole again in our body, mind, and spirit and are able to inspire others to participate in the activities for better health as well.
- Enhanced creativity: Detachment leads to a life of less, freeing up our mental bandwidth. With fewer distractions, disturbances, and elimination of noise, we are able to better channel our creative energy into worthwhile projects and pursuits. Addictions and attachments are leeches that keep sucking our creative energy and willpower. They leave us paralyzed as we part. As we let go of meaningless activities,

we are able to conserve our energy that we can focus on doing creative action. The haziness and cloudiness in our minds dissolve and the paralysis that was engulfing and stopping us from doing meaningful work goes away. We get our innate enthusiasm back. We can start with a few basic positive actions as we start our creative journey and soon, with consistency and persistence, we come up with plans, strategies, and avenues to fulfill our creative potential and work on positive and uplifting projects that serve humanity and leads to its betterment.

With knowledge of the immense benefits that come with detachment, it's a no-brainer that detachment is one of the best life skills that all of us can cultivate. With seductive forces lurking around us wherever we go, a commitment to detachment and letting go can prove to be a lifesaver for us.

In our finite human lives, in order to expand ourselves as well as have fun in our journeys, addictions and attachments are latent enemies that impede our experience. They are synonymous to Dementors that suck the life force out of us, making us cold-hearted and weak. To live the life of a victor, and a good human being, it is essential that we choose detachment and freedom over bondage and slavery. We have got one chance to live this human experience, then why not make good use of it? Why not make our stay on this rotating orb worthwhile and fun? Why not choose happiness and good health over despair, misery, and dis-ease?

Bettering ourselves in the present moments is much better than running after hours of lost time. I hope you choose a life of detachment and may freedom and happiness always be with you.

1

Imprisonment

Attachments

We all get attached to something our so or someone in our lives. Being attached is human nature, but once we understand why our brains prefer attachments over detachments, we can better be able to steer ourselves from the seductions of our everyday society and choose freedom over being imprisoned by our desires.

Attachment, unfortunately, is the cause of our suffering as well. We suffer more because the more things and people we get attached to, the more we start being burdened by worries, anxieties, resentment and other negative emotions. When we get attached to things external to us, we start getting identified by these things and objects. We lose vision of our higher purpose and deviate ourselves from living our truth so that we can satiate ourselves with the comfort and fulfillment of the desired objects. When we get more, we want more.

The core of every attachment and addiction is to feel a connection and to feel good. We are inundated with boring spaces and phases in our day-to-day life and don't what to do with our time. We feel a lack of stimulation. Our human brain wants excitement; it wants the rush to feel alive. All we are seeking is to bring life into our life again but the sad truth is we end up bringing things and entities into our lives that rob the life force out of us.

We want reassurance from external means that our life is still worth living. In this digital age, getting connected is easy and a few clicks away, but at the expense of genuineness and authenticity. We are chasing lies and running away from our inner personal truths. The solutions are not outside and in order to find them, we need to peek inside and know ourselves.

To know what truly excites us needs soul searching. It takes time, patience and an understanding of the bigger picture that all things are happening for a reason, a big reason that we are unable to see right now. Only then we will be able to connect the dots and uncover a lifestyle of detachment, extreme self-reliance and living our truth.

Addictions

The word 'addiction' is derived from a Latin term for 'enslaved by, or bound to'; addiction is akin to slavery and bondage. It is easy for our human brains to yearn for things from which we derive pleasure. Addictions have a great power to influence our brains that manifests in three avenues: craving for the object of addiction, loss of control while engaging in the activity, and consistent and continuous involvement in the activity despite awareness of the negative consequences that come with it.

In spite of knowing the fact that our aberrant behaviors are not helping us, we still engage in them. We throw our values, beliefs and health concerns and take high risks so that we can feed our cravings.

Addiction, whether big or small, is still an addiction. On a macro or micro scale, the truth is that we are all addicted to something extraneous or a particular behavior that helps us pacify.

During an addiction, we give up control and let our reckless behavior and misinformed state of mind control us. We become slaves to the ephemeral pleasures, turning into a hamster on the wheel repeating the same patterns, again and again, inching us towards insanity.

A big part of an addiction is the momentum behind it. We have invested a lot of our time, energy and resources in fulfilling our cravings. Our behavioral crutches have handicapped us from detaching from addictions. Moreover, we are scared of the void that will open up when we get rid of our addiction as we don't know how we will able to fill it. In essence, we fear our own success and well-being.

We need to understand that we have to slow down this momentum gradually and use our time effectively to pursue our other hobbies and interests. A great strategy is to incorporate meditation into our daily lives. Not only it calms us, but it also helps us get in alignment with our Inner Being. As we focus on spirituality and let go of the attachments of the body and the behaviors that come with the physical life, we become an observer and get an outsider's view of these patterns.

The worst part of addictions is the shame, guilt and the victim mindset that comes with it. We are so imprisoned by our own repeating patterns that we feel defeated and lost in the dark.

There are different kinds and forms of addictions that plague our current society. The leading and most common addictions that people in every stratum of society are dealing with are alcohol, nicotine, food, and drugs. Some other ones include the internet, shopping, hoarding, pornography, huffing, gambling, and sex.

Addiction recovery is not about cultivating abstinence from the things that we feel addicted to. It's about being mindful of consumption and intake. Often, we get so carried away that we lose control of ourselves.

Addictions don't go away easily and come with a heavy price. They are akin to Devil's Snare, the more we fight them, the more we get strangled. The process of recovery may take a long time and tons of willpower, but if we commit to it and get dialed into the reasons why we want to recover, i.e. tap into the *Why* power, we get inspired to embark on this journey. Addiction is a disease of body, mind, and soul, and our blind compulsions can take a toll on us.

There are several recovery programs such as Alcoholic Anonymous, Sex and Love Addicts Anonymous and similar associations where people get together, share their stories confidentially and help each other out in fighting addictions.

With technological advancements and ease of access, addictions are always going to be a threat to us. The best solution is to cultivate awareness, work on developing detachment and being prepared so that we can defend ourselves whenever the chains of addiction may try to bind us. With consistent self-introspection and feeding our minds with the right information, we will be able to protect our brains and shield our bodies from addictive objects and behaviors.

The Underlying Reason

The one-word answer to knowing why we get so drawn to addictions and attachments is dopamine. Many of us would have heard about it as it is the principal hormone responsible for inducing pleasure in us. Dopamine, not only is responsible for pleasure but also contributes to learning and memory. As a result, the brain records the stimulus and keeps craving for it.

Addictions and attachments activate the reward center in our brains using a shortcut mechanism thus flooding our brain with huge amounts of dopamine in an instant. Due to this, the brain gets easily hooked to engaging in addictive behaviors again and again. As the brain gets desensitized to dopamine levels, it craves more dopamine, thus starting a feedback loop that drives us to keep repeating the same behaviors.

In nature, rewards usually come only with time and effort. Addictive drugs and behaviors provide a shortcut, flooding the brain with dopamine and other neurotransmitters. With repetitive indulgence, the pleasure takes a backseat and obsession and compulsion kicks in.

It is useful to understand the underlying causes of addictive behaviors so that we can better decipher our motivations behind indulging in these poisonous behaviors.

- Mental issues: There is evidence that mental health issues and addictions go hand in hand. Often people with mental issues such as anxiety, depression, bipolar disorders, attention-deficit/hyperactivity disorder (ADHD) are drawn to stimuli that are addictive in nature. Addictions become coping mechanisms initially, but with repetitive indulgence, it leads to chronic problems. Both addictions and mental issues feed off each other and can significantly deteriorate a person's health if remain unchecked. On a minuscule scale, we all get anxious, stressed and depressed, and in those times, we must build habits that uplift our well-being rather than find refuge in addictions and external stimulus.

- Trauma: A deep-rooted link has been found between trauma and addiction. Trauma lies in the eye of the beholder and the nature of the traumatic event varies from person to person. For some, it may be fighting in a war, while for some it may be a car accident or a bad breakup. Every individual processes an unfortunate event in a different way. Trauma may cause the manifestation of mental issues, leading to involvement in addictive behaviors in order to cope.
- Sexual issues: Certain sexual apprehensions, may lead to addictions and uncontrollable attachments. Depending on how conservative the society is and how sexual freedom is practiced, individuals may suffer from various sexual issues. The LGBTQ community is at a higher risk due to challenging circumstances and a lack of acceptance. Shame and guilt may fuel these addictive behaviors leading to engagement in high-risk activities. Lack of comfort and confusion may drive people to get involved in substance abuse as well as different kinds of addictions to find relief. This backfires and leads to the manifestation of other mental health and serious issues. Sexual abuses during

childhood and traumatic events like rape may drive the victim to get involved with addictions. Because of the lack of communication and expression of piled-up feelings, addictions and attachments end up being a common avenue to deal with challenges.

- Negative Emotions: When people experience negative emotions such as fear, insecurity, jealousy, unworthiness, self-doubt, their self-esteem plummets down, and they become susceptible to get influenced by the seduction of addictions. Not feeling good leaves an unfillable void in a person, referred to as a 'hole in the soul' by the Big Book. The perception of the person gets flawed and hence the world starts to feel like a negative and hellish place. Addictions and attachments become the best ways to quench the thirst and fill this void in the person, but it always remains there driving the person to participate in ensuing negative and self-sabotaging behaviors.
- Boredom: The famous adage 'An idle mind is a devil's playground' is very true. Boredom can quickly become an easy excuse to engage in addictive behaviors. In reality, it is simply a manifestation of lack of purpose, inspiration, self-motivation and running out of creativity. People get imprisoned by the monotony of life and start feeling stuck in their lives, their jobs and relationships craving for novelty and escape. Instead of finding healthier alternatives to relieve this boredom, people start participating in anti-social and self-destructive behaviors that cause further pain, misery, and loneliness. In her post titled 'Boredom - a very real road to addiction' in Psychology Today, Carole Bennett writes, "Boredom is often simply a state of awareness that shows up just prior to the surfacing of difficult, painful

things we have stuffed away from our conscious awareness." Seeking thrills and adrenaline rush in high-risk activities may help us deal with boredom, but we end up paying a heavy price in the long run. Engaging in self-introspection and knowing what passions, interests, activities and events inspire us and make us happy can go a long way in spending quality time in worthwhile pursuits instead of feeling victimized and empty due to boredom. Open mind, optimism, and curiosity can be effective tools to overcome boredom and getting stuck in the mundane. We need to accept that boredom is a part of life and take responsibility for our actions. Finding strategies to tackle boredom will definitely help us in living a happier and healthier life.

2

Acceptance

The best starting point for us is acceptance. We need to take ownership of our attachments and addictions, and all the mistakes and bad karma we engaged in due to them. Many of us hide behind the shroud of denial pretending everything is fine in our lives. But deep down, we know how much harm it has caused us. We may be fine and look normal to others without an ounce of despair on our faces, but inside we suffer from pains, fears, and anxieties caused by our dependence on someone or something.

We need to let go of denial and face the truth… the truth that we are not living a life of authenticity and happiness. We need to wake up and take absolute ownership of the truth that we have been engulfed by the darkness and have lost our way. We need to accept the truth that we have become blinded by our own misaligned actions. Whether we like it or not, extreme ownership is only the way to move forward.

Taking Responsibility

We can spend countless hours blaming the circumstances or other people for our addictions and attachments. But there was only one thing that got us down into the rabbit hole: our lack of judgment. We are 100% responsible for our actions and for the consequent mistakes that we have made. In the book *The Compound Effect*, Darren Hardy has expressed this notion beautifully in these words: "No matter what has happened to you, take complete responsibility for it—good or bad, victory or defeat. Own it."

We may have hurt people closest to us under the influence of external stimuli, without intending to do so. But brooding over the past, repeating our mistakes and feeling shame and guilt inside us will not take us far. If we keep wondering what went wrong and keep dissecting and overanalyzing things and events we will always be stuck in the loop. Instead of blaming, we need to foster responsibility.

We're responsible for everything that we have done so far. Yes, we screwed up. Yes, we made a mess. By taking responsibility, we reclaim the power to ourselves. We remind ourselves again that we are in control. We get out of the daze and the ensuing foggy behaviors.

The instructions that we give ourselves are: *No complaints. No excuses. No blame*. These are simple on paper, but difficult to execute. If we want to bring a powerful change in our lives, we need to take responsibility. Jim Rohn has said, "You must take personal responsibility. You cannot change the circumstances, the seasons, or the wind, but you can change yourself."

Taking responsibility and acknowledging our mistakes is not

an act of weakness, it is an act of strength. Instead of being afraid of other people's judgments and flooding ourselves with shame, and guilt, we need to own up and stand tall. There's no point in getting bogged down because it will keep us stagnant. In order to move and be able to progress we need to take absolute responsibility for our past aberrant behaviors. Only then, we will be able to march forward and envision a life of power and dignity.

Becoming Vulnerable

Vulnerability is a tough choice, to make, but it comes with the maximum benefits. Brené Brown has remarked: "Owning our story can be hard but not nearly as difficult as spending our lives running from it. Embracing our vulnerabilities is risky but not nearly as dangerous as giving up on love and belonging and joy—the experiences that make us the most vulnerable. Only when we are brave enough to explore the darkness will we discover the infinite power of our light."

Vulnerability is opening up ourselves and our scars and wounds to others. It may come with pain and resistance but if we look at the overall picture, it is beneficial and has a long-term positive impact on us.

We are letting down the walls around us and we are exposing our true nature. When we let go of the fear of judgment and shame, we not only allow others to help us, but most importantly we allow ourselves to help us. Our irrational and baseless fears can stop us from living our life fully. The dual lives that we have been living are costing us our health, our well-being and our relationships. We need to open ourselves. As much as we hate and feel scared, this needs to be done.

Choosing vulnerability may seem like wearing a cloak of weakness, but it is in fact a cape of courage. To make deeper connections and relationships in our lives, we need to become vulnerable. We need to stop the pretense and gimmickry that we have been showing to the world. We need to detach from the various masks that we have been wearing. We always pay heavy prices when we compromise our authenticity for ephemeral validation and rewards. Embrace yourself and know that becoming vulnerable is your best step towards a shift, in yourself and your life.

The most important thing to realize is that you're not alone! There are countless people all around the world who are experiencing the same pain, suffering and stirred emotions, just like you. Vulnerability is a prerequisite to be able to reach others and let others reach you, so that everyone can get together, share their experiences and uplift each other.

3

Shift

Surrendering

Once we accept our reality and have zero ounces of denial and regret in ourselves, that's when a shift starts to happen. The first part of any powerful change that we want to go through is surrendering. We, human beings, like to be in control of our destiny and our life, but things and circumstances change. We may not be as powerful and invincible as we think we are. The clarity will only come when we surrender and know that all we have to do is do our best. There will be times of difficulties and moments of weakness and no matter how much we try to resist them, they will always persist.

When our patterns and vices overpower us, our resistance is futile. The most effective thing we can do during those times is to surrender. This may seem counterintuitive but letting go always takes us eventually to a position of strength and reclaiming our power.

Making a shift is not easy as our previous behaviors and patterns have an immense momentum behind them. To paraphrase Abraham, the momentum of our thoughts is similar to the momentum of a train going in one direction. In order for us to get the train going in the other direction, our first step is to slow down the momentum of this train. Once the train comes to a halt, that's when we can start building momentum gradually in the other direction.

As we surrender, we start slowing down the momentum of our compulsive thoughts and actions. Once we come to a place of stillness, we can gently nudge ourselves towards alignment. As our inner calm gets restored and we get aligned, we can start treading in the direction of our well-being and eventually create a massive shift in our lives.

Seeking Alignment

The main reason for this out of whack life that we are living currently is because we have derailed from our true purpose and essence. We are no longer in tune with our happiness, our inner strength, and our true core self. We may get a glimpse of it now and then, but the perennial flow of our authenticity has been blocked due to our addictions and attachments.

As we go through these tumultuous times, we need to understand that the first step to restoring ourselves and bettering our lives is seeking alignment again. We don't have to wait for a seemingly 'opportune' time for us to get better. This is a sign of procrastination and it is a weakness. Delaying our well-being for someday in the future won't serve us. Now is the day, when we need to work on reinstating our alignment again.

There are many avenues that we can choose to seek alignment. Some of them are meditation, praying, making a list of the positive aspects of a life without the addiction or attachment we are struggling with, and visualizing our ideal life and internalizing the destination that we are trying to go to.

Once we have a clear vision and activate the 'WHY power' within us, that's when we are able to reclaim a sense of purpose again. Previously, we were not plugged in and there was neither electricity nor energy that was powering us. But now, as we seek and get back into alignment with the Infinite intelligence and the Wiser Being within us, we start taking steps towards a happy and free life.

Alignment comes with repetition and grit, and by cultivating new, better habits on a day-to-day basis. We need to design new routines and rituals that when done daily keep us grounded in our natural sense of well-being. Once we get aligned and get back on track, we need to continue gathering this new momentum and build systems that keep us balanced. Initially, it may take a lot of effort for us and we need to keep feeding ourselves with positivity and good, useful information, but once we are able to get habituated to a new healthier way of living, then life will go on an upward spiral again easily and effortlessly.

Changing Our Perception

As we get aligned, we undergo the most important shift that we need, a shift in perception. It's all a matter of discarding our previous lens and looking at life through a new one. It's fascinating how we start viewing people, events and circumstances around us in a completely different way. The world is still the same, but it's our newfound perception that compels us to see it in a new light. Marcus Aurelius echoed this sentiment in one of his reflections: "Today I escaped anxiety. Or no, I discarded it, because it was within me, in my own perceptions — not outside."

Addiction is often referred to as a disease of perception. Because it has mainly affected the way we see ourselves and the world around us, it may take some time and awareness for us to get back to the healthy perception that we are born with. The Stoics teach that by controlling our perceptions, we can attain mental peace and clarity. A change in perception, along with discipline and a strong Why, will fuel us again towards reclaiming our power and our life and get us started on the path to redemption.

We need to start believing that everything in this world is temporary, When we believe in impermanence, especially of our addictive behaviors, and the hold that our attachments have on us will decay with time, we start believing in recovery, and awaken hope within us. We get in tune with our authentic selves and start discerning what objects, desires, and choices take us towards recovery and which ones keep us stuck.

Making Hard Choices

As we get aligned and start getting back on track, and as we start seeing a shift in our patterns, we come face-to-face with some hard choices. These are choices that we need to make, that may make us feel like we are swimming against the current, but if we look at a broader picture, they actually help us in changing our orientation so that we start swimming along with the bigger and more natural flow: the flow of our well-being. We flow with the Source, the infinite intelligence within us.

For a short time, we need to restrict and restrain our reckless selves and go through a phase of non-doing. We need to rely on the parachute till we land safely. It may be easy to shift some patterns, but for the extreme and resilient we may need to use extreme measures. The choices will be difficult, but if we are dialed in with our intentions and the reasoning is clear, then we will plow through those obstacles.

It's all a matter of choosing short-term pleasure over long-term happiness. Once our actions start aligning with our newly discovered core values and principles, making hard choices will be a no-brainer. We will learn how to tackle our inner fears, restlessness, and anxieties. Our suffering is not futile, but it has a great meaning behind it. We are fighting for ourselves. As Victor Frankl has said, "In some ways suffering ceases to be suffering at the moment it finds a meaning, such as the meaning of a sacrifice."

Pivoting is not easy but we will keep reaping recurrent rewards once we go through this shift. We don't need to suffer for lost and unnecessary causes. Essentially, we are putting an end to the sufferings that our addictions and attachments have caused in us, and choosing a 'better' suffering of committing to hard choices. The latter suffering that we will be going through is ephemeral but with a long-lasting impact. When we start focusing on impact and let go of our pleasures, that's when we bring a powerful change in ourselves and our lives.

When we make hard choices, we regain our long-lost self-esteem, dignity and reclaim our personal power. We embark on the journey from pain to power. We strengthen our muscle of willpower. The hold that external objects and situations have had on us withers away, and we become prepared and ready to go through any challenges that our life may put us through. As the modern Stoic Jerzy Gregorek has quite succinctly put this truth in the following words: "Hard choices, easy life. Easy choices, hard life."

Trusting a Higher Power

We have evidence of a Higher Power all around us. There is an intelligence that is way beyond the comprehension of the human mind. When we are struggling with our addictions and attachments and not able to overcome them, we may feel powerless and weak. In those times, we can rely on a Higher Power that is present in all of us. Nature has created and designed a broad spectrum of living entities on the planet with the utmost precision and we, humans, are its masterpiece. We are miracles, to say the least. We can again rely on that latent power that drives us, and seek wisdom, clarity, and well-being from the Source.

It does not matter what we call this Higher Power - we

may call it God, Infinite Intelligence, *logos,* Almighty or the Supreme Soul - we need to know that we have a presence of this power within us. Because of our physical and psychological problems, we get into the perception that we are mere frail humans walking on Earth. But we are spiritual in nature. We are eternal beings. As Wayne Dyer has said, "We are not human beings in search of a spiritual experience. We are spiritual beings immersed in a human experience."

As we are spiritual beings, our healing and solutions also need to be spiritual. We need divine interventions to restore us to our well-being. The group Alcoholics Anonymous is has been transparent about the fact that a 'vital spiritual experience' is necessary for recovery. Step 2 of the Twelve Steps is: We came to believe that a power greater than ourselves could restore us to sanity.

We need to change our vantage point and undergo an 'identity transplantation.' The obstacles that we may face are the monkey mind (the incessant chatter that does not help us), our numb heart (that is depriving us of experiencing love, connection and the beautiful feelings that we are not able to experience), and our physical body (that is tethered to our compulsive actions, tying us to a caged, malignant existence).

We have failed and now we need to surrender to the Higher Power to help us in our healing process. We have tarnished our minds, hearts, and bodies with addictions and attachments. Even if we have lost all our capacity to trust others and hope for a better life, we can rely on the absolute intelligence within us and let it take charge. We need to open our minds and hearts and become solution-oriented rather than being problem-focused.

Thomas Keating, in his book *Divine Therapy and Addiction*, has said, "The love of God or the Higher Power is what heals us. Nobody becomes a full human being without love. It brings to life people who are most damaged. The steps are really an engagement in an ever-deepening relationship with God. Divine love picks us up when we sincerely believe nobody else will. We then begin to experience freedom, peace, calm, equanimity, and liberation from cravings for what we have come to know are damaging — cravings that cannot bring happiness, but at best only momentary relief that makes the real problem worse."

4

Healing

Asking for Help

No matter how invincible or strong we feel we are, the truth is we are not. We need others. In this journey of life, becoming a solo traveler for an extended period of time can prove to be toxic for us. We, humans, get an immense value from sharing with others. We are driven to offer help to others, but when we want help for ourselves, we step back. We are afraid of being perceived as weak. We feel shameful and guilty to share our darkest obsessions and our toxic compulsive behaviors.

We shut ourselves out, and think that cocooning ourselves from the world while we work on improving ourselves is the right thing to do. But it is not! Now is the time when we need to reach out to someone and share our feelings with that person. Friends and family are there to support us, but it's a better idea to share the things that are bothering you with someone who can advise you and at the same time you feel safe to confide in. This person can be a therapist, a spiritual leader or teacher, the religious head of your temple, church, mosque or any institution that you are a part of. There are no hard rules.

We need guidance to be able to restore our self-esteem and our well-being. We need someone to pick us from the hole that we have dug ourselves in. There is nothing shameful to seek help. In fact, it's an act of courage. We communicate that we are aware of our current state and are hopeful that change can be made in our lives. We express our vulnerability and choose to be transparent and let go of the secrecy that has been burdening us for so long.

When we ask for help we are actually moving in a direction that supports our vision. We let go of the fears that have been stopping us from taking measurable actions. Because we are in a position where we feel powerless, we need someone who helps us restore the confidence that we once had in ourselves. We need to be able to monitor our progress and regain the control we have over our own actions.

Even if we have been betrayed by people whom we trusted, we need to believe that there are still tons of people that can shower us with love, care and understand our situation. If we approach the right people and let go of our fears, inhibitions, and apprehensions we take a step towards change. Changing our minds and changing situations is hard, but with a step-by-step approach and potent guidance, we can morph our lives to becoming better. Help is always available, we need to reach out, and be able to trust again.

Setting Healthy Boundaries

Often, getting attached to something or someone means that we have failed to create and maintain healthy boundaries for ourselves. As an act of self-deception, we delay forming boundaries around our behaviors. We think boundaries mean sacrificing and giving up our freedom. We fantasize about discipline but at the same time, it means we will need to let go of our previous aberrant behaviors. This is hard. Although it sounds paradoxical, setting healthy boundaries is a key to freedom.

Sometimes, even with multiple attempts, we fail at changing our patterns. We get frustrated at trying to bring about positive change in our lives. We are not yet convinced to our core that our attachments and addictions are not actually comforting and soothing or pacifying us, but are mere sources of pain and suffering. In those times, in order to restore balance in the long run, we need to take some extreme actions. As the popular adage goes: Desperate times, desperate measures.

Before we take any action, we need to seek alignment first by making a list of positive aspects of letting go of an attachment or addiction. For instance, if you are wanting to quit smoking, then write down all the positive aspects of committing to it. As we refer to these positive aspects on a daily basis, we need to take extreme actions and let go of the addiction cold turkey.

If you can't resist chocolate or ice cream, don't bring them in your house. Guard the doors of your home and become a gatekeeper. Zero in on your temptations and stay away from them. Have a window of commitment, maybe 30 days, 90 days or as long as you can. We need time for the power within us to heal us and rewire our brains.

Make your body, your home and your personal space a fortress. Even if it aches and is not easy and divorcing yourself from food, drugs, alcohol, porn, or a toxic friendship or relationship may cause immense pain and unimaginable withdrawal symptoms, we need to know that this is an important step we need to take. The pain and suffering are temporary and a one-time price that we need to pay in order to restore our sanity and reclaim our power.

We need to understand that we are setting these boundaries not only for bettering ourselves, but also for bettering the lives of the people around us.

Overcoming Obsessions and Compulsions

We are all obsessed with something or the other. The problem occurs when we go aboard. For instance, letting work seep into the cracks of our leisure time. Whenever we experience boredom, we seek novelty by doing some behavior that we think will cause us relief. We get on the train of repeating these behaviors again and again. What started as our choice is no longer a choice for us, it's a repetitive pattern over which we have lost control. In essence, the momentum behind that habit or behavior is so strong, that we feel that our obsessive and compulsive behaviors are a way of life for us, and we cannot change them.

Our obsessions and compulsive behaviors do pacify us momentarily, but they also rob us of our vitality and happiness. No matter how much we try to control and manage these patterns, without external help and guidance, it may take a long time for us to dispose of these sabotaging behaviors.

The root causes of these obsessions and compulsions are fears that are deep-rooted within our subconscious that we may not be even aware of. These fears rule our behaviors and we remain stuck in the same pattern. Seeking solutions to interrupt these patterns is important to make progress. While there is no potent cure for our obsessions and compulsions, we need to cultivate new behaviors that can form new neural pathways in our brains.

As laid out by Charles Duhigg in his iconic book, *The Power of Habit*, habits have a system of cue and reward. The habit loop starts with a cue, whether it is situational or emotional, followed by a behavior that gives us some kind of reward. It is analogous to the sensation of an itch, doing the required behavior which is scratching that leads us to the reward of relief.

Once we observe and identify the cue, we need to change the behavior by doing something else, and see if it gives us the same reward. If the new behavior does not provide us with the same reward, we need to experiment with another one, and keep experimenting until we are able to figure out a new behavior, thus re-establishing a new healthier habit loop.

For instance, many of us seek porn as a refuge when we feel lonely or bored. We are seeking both connection and relief, those are our rewards. We need to take a healthier journey so that we are able to reach the same destination and get our rewards without any harm to us. Here, the routines or behaviors that we have adopted are compulsive porn consumption and the ensuing addiction to masturbation and orgasm. As the dopamine kicks in, we feel relieved and satisfied but that is momentary, and soon we are again craving for more of it. Also, the connection that we are seeking is void fundamentally as we are only stimulated by pixelated screens and hence there is no real connection. To overcome this compulsive behavior is to switch it with a healthier one. Some alternatives, for instance, in this case, would be seeking authentic connections with people who are like-minded and/or are trying to overcome the same challenge, thus going to Sex and Love Addicts Anonymous meetings and joining online forums where we are able to share our thoughts and connect with other people. Through revealing our concerns and talking them out we can find relief as well. Other alternatives are meditating to seek and establish a connection with the Higher Power or participating in a creative endeavor such as painting. With repetition, we will be able to replace our old behavioral patterns with new healthier ones and the rewards will be of better quality and exponentially long-lasting.

Because the momentum of our compulsory and obsessive thoughts is so strong, we need to start making a list of all the positive aspects of living a life without these compulsions. So, for the above instance, we can list all the great things that will happen if we quit porn consumption and get rid of our addiction to masturbation. Some benefits may include having more time for ourselves, an increase in energy and vitality, more meaningful connections, and better focus and clarity. Reading this list consistently will keep us on track to overcome addictive habits and designing a new future for ourselves.

In the end, it's all about looking at the bigger picture and choosing long-term gains over momentary pleasures, and trusting the power within us.

5

Freedom

From Victim to Victor

Our attachments and addictions keep us entrapped and because we lose grip over our own behaviors, we feel we have lost all control. We become victimized. We think life is happening to us and our fate is decided. There is no way the tables can be turned and we are doomed. The more we try to escape the life outside, the more the life inside us escapes. When we get seduced by victimhood, we lose our power. Every human has an untapped power inside him or her and if we are not aligned with it, we start believing that we are just frail Earthlings not good for anything and just passing time and tolerating the sequence of events that happen in our lives. Victimhood is not an option for us. Every story of recovery and redemption begins with a choice, a choice to become a victor and take control of our life.

Victimhood gives us the incentive of using as many excuses as we can because we get the 'pass' to live an easy and lazy life. It fuels our addictions, our obsessions, and compulsions, and we get inside the negativity loop never getting better. Becoming a victor from a victim demands a tiny but monumental shift in perspective: instead of feeling that life is happening to us, we need to start thinking life is happening for us. We need to believe that we are constantly expanding and growing.

Our past is gone and can never be changed, but today is a gift. What we do today will determine our future. We need to take care of ourselves today. As we start the transition, we need to take small baby steps. The progress will be slow but we need to continue walking on the path of change with grit and perseverance. By making tiny shifts in our thoughts, actions and choosing better habits, we will emerge victorious. The journey from baby steps to a victory lap is not easy; we may stumble and fall again and again but each obstacle will make us strong and more focused.

Jack Canfield in his book *The Success Principles* explains that we need to take 100% responsibility for our lives. We need to let go of blame, excuses, and complaints. They are toxic to our lives and our success. In our journey to relief, recovery, and freedom, we will need to feed our minds constantly with positivity and hope. Having heroes and referring to their success stories will create a spark of change in ourselves as well as raise our vibrational capital. As we become certain of success and freedom, we will gain the lost confidence in ourselves. Thinking of our past victories will help us connect with the Inner Hero that has always been there within us. Now is the time to shed dormancy and awaken this giant being. There is no point in living the life of a victim. As we make the choice to become a victor, we let go of self-deception and start cultivating self-reliance. The path to glory is never easy, but with the right tools in our arsenal, we can win this battle. Let's get going, victory awaits you!

Becoming a Giver

When we are attached or addicted, whether we are conscious or not, we become takers. We start feeding off other people or things to satisfy our urges. We think happiness comes from transactions, and that tempts us to participate in actions that we later regret. But as we work hard on ourselves and redeem ourselves, we claim our power back and enrich our capacity to give.

We need to commit to acts of generosity, it doesn't matter whether they are big or small. The perks of becoming a giver are both physiological and psychological. Truth be told, between a giver and receiver, it is the giver who benefits the most. There is plenty of evidence that supports how generosity can have a positive impact on various facets of our well-being as well as others. It's important we understand these benefits to better able to nurture a giving and compassionate attitude within us.

Mindset

A 2008 Harvard study found that giving money to someone else instead of spending it on ourselves lifted participants' happiness.

Sonja Lyubomirsky, a professor of psychology at the University of California, Riverside observed similar outcomes when she asked people to perform five acts of kindness each week for six weeks. Another study in 2006 conducted by Jorge Moll and his colleagues at the National Institutes of Health concluded that when people give to charity, it activated the regions of the brain that are associated with pleasure, trust and social connection. This was backed by researchers at the Stony Brook University, as they found that generosity released several chemicals in the brain causing inner joy and tranquility. This phenomenon was termed as 'giver's glow.' Giving activates the reward circuitry in our brains. Scientists believe that philanthropy and altruistic behavior causes the release of happiness chemicals such as dopamine, serotonin, oxytocin, and endorphins, producing a positive feeling called 'helper's high'. Hence, happiness gets reflected in our biology and lights us up.

Healthset

The fascinating thing about giving is that it helps you live longer. Researchers suggest that the main reason giving may improve physical health and longevity is that it helps reduce stress levels, which are associated with a plethora of health problems. In a 2006 study jointly conducted by Johns Hopkins University and the University of Tennessee, it was observed that participants who provided social support to others had lower blood pressure than the ones who didn't. A 2013 study at the Carnegie Mellon University found similar results. They found that people who volunteer around four hours a week are

40% less likely to develop high blood pressure than the ones who didn't. These findings show a direct correlation between giving and health, hence inferring that generosity comes with physiological advantages, hence a win-win situation for both the giver and the receiver.

Stephanie Brown and her colleagues from the University of Michigan have found that people who provided practical help to friends, relatives or neighbors, or gave emotional comfort and support to their spouses had a lower risk of dying over a five year period than the ones who didn't. In his book *Why Good Things Happen to Good People*, Stephen Post, Professor of Family, Population and Preventive Medicine at Stony Brook University confirms that generosity and giving increases health benefits in patients with chronic illnesses such as HIV and multiple sclerosis.

Giving is a great antidote to depression, which affects millions of people around the world. Data obtained from Project MATCH, a comprehensive alcoholism treatment trial, reveals that people in Alcoholics Anonymous double their chances of success when they help others. Helping others is analogous to teaching and the more we help others, the more we learn about ourselves and hence the more we are able to help ourselves. This is a good indication that giving may help people overcome other kinds of addictions as well, along with its benefits in the spectrum of disorders and diseases.

Heartset

Along with the benefits of becoming happier and healthier, giving also promotes social connection and bonding. Giving leads to social interdependence, which unlike attachment is unconditional and reciprocal in nature. When we give to others, not only do they feel closer to us as a result, but we feel closer to them as well. In her book *The How of Happiness,* Sonja Lyubomirsky writes: "Being kind and generous leads you to perceive others more positively and more charitably, and this fosters a heightened sense of interdependence and cooperation in your social community."

Acts of generosity and service trigger mirror neurons in our brains. It doesn't matter if the act of giving is a small or big one. For instance, even if you smile at the people who you meet and come across, whether it be at your workplace, on the street, or at a mall, they smile back at you. This is due to the triggering of mirror neurons.

Mirror neurons get activated and stimulated not only when we perform an act of generosity but also when we observe someone else doing such an act. The beauty of these neurons is that just by looking at someone else's face, we are able to interpret the emotions that they are going through. They help us put ourselves in other people's shoes. As we are able to better relate to them, we can help them and as we offer our service and the person receives it, both ourselves and the other person feel better, again by stimulation of the neurons. A fascinating finding is that if someone else watches you doing an act of kindness, the mirror neurons in that person respond as well benefitting that person too. Hence, mirror neurons are indispensable in cultivating empathy within us that inspires us to participate in the act of generosity and as a result creating a feedback loop of positive emotions not only in the giver, i.e. us, and the receiver but also in the observer enhancing the well-being of everyone involved.

Once we realize how our moods and actions can affect other people and vice versa, we can guide ourselves to become more giving, kind and compassionate. When we give, it's a win-win situation for everyone.

Giving should never be done in exchange for any favors and we don't need to tie any expectations or outcomes when we give. When we give unconditionally, that's when the magic happens.

People enjoy spending time with people who are giving and compassionate. The best-kept secret about forming and forging any kind of relationship, whether it be professional or personal, is that we need to be givers. As we give more, we are likely to get more back. Several studies suggest that when we give to others, we are likely to be rewarded by others down the line — either by the person you gave to or by someone else. These exchanges promote a sense of trust and cooperation strengthening the bond. In his book *Loneliness: Human Nature and the Need for Social Connection,* researcher John Cacioppo writes: "The more extensive the reciprocal altruism born of social connection… the greater the advance toward health, wealth, and happiness."

Soulset

Giving evokes a sense of gratitude not only in the receiver but also in the giver. The more we give, the more we cultivate the belief that this world is a place for us to create, not compete. The more we give, the more we are inspired to focus on our genius and our potential. We come in alignment with our higher self and our Inner Being.

Giving is an act of power. The gifts that we give open the portals of different realms through which abundance can flow to us. When we give, we are not only able to dissolve the mindset of scarcity and lack in the receiver, but most importantly in ourselves. As both the giver and receiver cultivate gratitude with regard to the gifts given and received, it leads both of them towards positivity and feeling good. Research has found that gratitude plays an instrumental role in health, prosperity, social bonds, and happiness and contentment.

When we open our hands to give, we also put ourselves in the receiving mode. The Universe has its ways of bringing abundance to us when we engage in altruism. When we give, we activate the flow of abundance to and through us. As we get in this flow, we become an instrument, a conduit if you will, of bringing beautiful creations into the world. When we give, we are bound to get exponential returns over time.

Giving brings a big paradigm shift to us. If we are seeking abundance in an area of our lives — whether it be wealth, health, relationships — we can end our struggle by giving more. As Zig Ziglar has said, "You can have everything in life you want if you will just help enough other people get what they want."

As we give, we change the lens through which we see this

world and start perceiving it as a place of cooperation and not competition. We eject ourselves out of the race. We get rid of comparisons and over-analytical behaviors As Maya Angelou has remarked, "I have found that among its other benefits, giving liberates the soul of the giver."

Through generosity, we are able to tap into the feeling of appreciation and as a result, connect in a better way with the Higher Power. We direct ourselves towards clarity and become in tune with our purpose. Through meaningful creations and contributions, we enrich our souls. Through giving and the ensuing feeling of appreciation, we are able to attain inner peace and tranquility. We are able to attain a true sense of freedom.

In essence, with our spiritual expansion, we raise our vibrations and are able to give in bigger and better ways, thus serving humanity in ways that we never thought were possible for us.

The best part about giving is that it is contagious. The ripple effect that we create through our acts of generosity has the potential to impact countless lives. It's similar to initiating a chain reaction. Even with our seemingly small acts of giving and kindness, we have the potential to spread positivity and happiness to not only one person but many others. With the advent of the Internet and technology, our giving is no longer limited by the constraints of time and space.

Giving has never been easier, and we are living in an era where we can sharpen and nourish our generosity easily and effortlessly. As people all around the world are able to witness our generosity and get inspired by our acts of giving, we are truly blessed to be surrounded by an abundance of opportunities to impact innumerable lives across the planet.

Studies show that when one person behaves altruistically, it inspires the observer to also participate in acts of generosity.

With social media and other tools at our disposal, our altruism can impact not only the people in our network, but also hundreds or thousands of people that we have never met. Through a spark of our generosity, we can create a raging fire of hope and change and provide relief and assistance to the less privileged people.

So whether you buy gifts, donate money to a charity whose cause aligns with you, or volunteer at a local non-profit organization, your generosity can begin a cascade of long-lasting impact and upliftment. As we give more, we are able to improve our mindset, healthset, heartset and soulset and influence countless lives. We are able to make this world a better place, serve humanity and attain inner peace and personal freedom that has always for some reason eluded us.

As the popular adage goes 'Giving is living,' the more we help others, the more we end up helping ourselves. There is no better life than one of a giver. It's your time to cherish your newfound freedom and use it for the betterment of others. We are counting on you!

Daily Disciplines

Our success lies in our daily disciplines. We can channel our obsessions and compulsions towards doing daily rituals and routines that help us grow and attract abundance and success. In the words of Jocko Willink, 'Discipline equals freedom.' We need to be in consistent touch with sources that help us becoming our higher selves.

By letting go of our codependent patterns, keeping ourselves on track and committing to a disciplined lifestyle every single day, we can bring positive changes in our lives. An excellent way is to feed positive information to our minds daily. Whatever challenge you are dealing with, it's likely that other people have faced similar challenges and overcome them and through these stories, we can keep ourselves inspired. Books are can be our great friends and comrades in this journey. I personally love books that have short daily meditations that I can read every day. I highly recommend *The Daily Stoic* by Ryan Holiday and Stephen Hanselman and *The Language of Letting Go* by Melody Beattie. Reading these books is effortless and helps us keep aligned and enjoy our freedom. When we trust philosophy and believe that the Universe has our back, we are able to liberate ourselves.

Morning routines that are effective and help us start our days on the right foot can be instrumental in building the right momentum for our days. Daily disciplines such as meditaton, journaling, exercise, yoga, positive affirmations, visualization, reading and learning can be great in cultivating virtues and inching towards our ideal future. Day by day, by virtue of the Compound Effect, we can create personal expansion and change our lives.

In essence, true freedom is when we enjoy the journey and let go of the destinations. If we cultivate the discipline of doing the things that make us feel good about ourselves and our life, we make our journey more enjoyable and fun.

So let go, lighten up, build daily disciplines and start having fun and enjoying your well-deserved freedom. Your time has come!

6

Conclusion

Life is all about drifting between two polarities: birth and death, action and rest, good and evil, and detachment and desire.

We may choose extremity for a while but if left unchecked, it always leads to misery, whether we are completely detached or filled with desires. We need to steer ourselves and be the captain of our souls. We may start with an initial goal of surviving, but our attention should always be directed towards thriving… and thriving well! In order to live a good life, we need to be able to seek balance. We may have lived in a cage for so long that we have conditioned ourselves to ignore the abundance and opulence that is always there for us. We may have forgotten the virtues of well-being, happiness, and true joy.

The paradox of detachment is that it needs to be a warm and cozy place for us where we can seek refuge for a while, but we also need to get back to life and address our desires as well. When we face the winters of life, we can live in a comfortable cottage that helps us in healing and restoring our well-being, but we know we need to get back out there and fight a good fight. The human mind is expansive, and as we live, we will invite new desires in ourselves. There's no going around this truth. But we need to be able to know when we need to draw a line in the sand.

We can learn lessons from our past where we may have engaged in extreme behaviors and figure out how to live a life of balance and equilibrium. We learn how our attachments and addictions cause misery and suffering essentially caging us. Those patterns of codependence and negligence of our well-being and personal freedom cost us hefty amounts. Our time, attention, energy and other resources that were spent on feeding those desires won't come back, but once we surrender, accept our flaws and commit to rebooting our lives, we make a powerful change. The alignment that we attain through detachment helps us tap into our personal power. As we align, we get ready to birth new desires that have the potential to bring more virtues and well-being not only for ourselves but for others as well.

Through a life of intentionality and essentialism, we can start focusing on the right desires for us and detach from the ones that don't serve us. There is no better life than that of a self-reliant person. We live a life enriched with love and connection and severe all chains of empty satisfactions. Our actions are no longer stained with expectations. Our ego has no power for us.

Detachment is not a one-time quick fix, it is a lifestyle. We need to tap into our inner guidance and know when we need to detach and when we don't need to. We need to be aware of the healthy attachments and desires as well and drift towards them when we need to. In the end, it's all about maneuvering ourselves and going with the flow as we go through the journey of our lives.

By raising our standards and letting go of unhealthy expectations, we can design a life of contentment, one that is whole in every aspect. Once we look at the bigger picture and trust that we will be able to connect the dots in the future, we will start making hard choices and detaching from what does not serve us. What we are seeking is already within us — once we realize this truth, we are able to let go and attain happiness, peace, and inner tranquility and live a life of ease and freedom.

"Detachment is not the absence of emotion, it is the process of becoming one with the Oneness that is the Universe. To be detached, is to realize that the fullness of all there is, is too much to react to with just one emotion, one thought, or any bias. To be detached, is to acknowledge all, without owning any of it. To be detached, is to summon forth the whole entirety of understanding, to the fragment that is the void."

— Justin K. McFarlane Beau

"Detachment involves "present moment living" — living in the here and now. We allow life to happen instead of forcing and trying to control it. We relinquish regrets over the past and fears about the future. We make the most of each day."

— Melody Beattie

If you think this book has added value to you and helped you in any way, please consider giving a copy to your loved ones, family members, coworkers, friends or someone you just met, whom you care about and want greater success for. When we help others and give away our time, earnings, and most importantly our heart, the ripple effect ends up bringing more abundance and prosperity to us.

To read more useful material on how to create an extraordinary life and become a better version of yourself every day, please visit my website:

ParthSawhney.com

ABOUT THE AUTHOR

Parth Sawhney is an author and success mentor to high-achievers all around the world. Through his writing and artworks, he shares ideas, insights and resources related to personal development, philosophy, success psychology and the human condition. His recent books include *The Daily Apple, Thriving in the New Normal*, *The Way of the Karma Yogi*, and *The Detachment Manifesto*. When he is not working, Parth enjoys spending time in coffee shops and taking long walks.

www.ingramcontent.com/pod-product-compliance
Ingram Content Group UK Ltd.
Pitfield, Milton Keynes, MK11 3LW, UK
UKHW042000190726
13854UKWH00005B/2081

9 798201 483326